The Fight for Lithuanian Independence: The History and Legacy of Lithuania in the 20th Century

By Charles River Editors

A picture of an anti-Soviet rally in Lithuania

Introduction

A picture of the Baltic Way rally against Soviet occupation

Modern day Lithuania is a small country bordering the Baltic Sea with a population of less than 3 million people, but despite its relative size, the nation has exerted an influential role on the history of the region. More recently, in the 20th century, Lithuania was caught between much larger powers in two world wars and then the Cold War. Along with neighbors Latvia and Estonia, Lithuania was one of the only states to truly break free of the Soviet Union when the latter dissolved in 1991. Now entrenched in the EU's political and security bloc, Lithuania has seen unprecedented economic growth and prosperity, although Vilnius is still wary of the Russian giant on its doorstep.

The end of the Cold War brought Lithuania the independence it had sought for almost 200 years and had only briefly attained in the 1918-39 Interwar Period. This is due in large measure to its location, as Lithuania is wedged between Poland and the Russian exclave of Kaliningrad to the south, Belarus to the east and Latvia to the north. The country's capital city is Vilnius and next largest city is Kaunas. Covering an area of 65,000 square kilometers, although at various stages of its history this was much greater, Lithuania borders the Baltic Sea to the west. Indeed, it is perhaps best to think of the country as a Baltic one, and as with the other Baltic states, Lithuania has been at the crossroads of events involving European, Middle Eastern, and Asian powers. For centuries, its main relationships were with Poland, Sweden, and the burgeoning Rus peoples, later Russia and Ukraine. Subsequently Germany would become an important player in the Baltics, while Russia's Romanov dynasty coveted access to the Baltic sea lanes, inevitably meaning Lithuania would come into its sights.

Given everything going on around it, it should come as little surprise that Lithuania's history during the 20th century revolved around the remarkable resilience of its people in the face of aggression and imperialism from first Russia, then Nazi Germany, then the Soviet Union.

The Fight for Lithuanian Independence: The History and Legacy of Lithuania in the 20th Century examines the geopolitics of the region, Lithuania's place in it, and the most important events in Lithuania's recent history. Along with pictures depicting important people, places, and events, you will learn about Lithuania like never before.

World War I

Lithuania was not always a small country up against larger, more aggressive ones. Inhabitants in the region date back tens of thousands of years but the first recognizable Lithuanians were recorded by history in about 1000 CE. The Grand Duchy of Lithuania developed in the following centuries to become the region's powerhouse, at one stage ruling from the Baltic Sea to the Black Sea. Indeed, Lithuania was Europe's largest state in the 14th century. It was the relationship with Poland that solidified Lithuania's place in European history in the centuries after the Middle Ages. The two neighboring countries formed the Polish-Lithuanian Commonwealth in 1569 and survived until the late 18th century as one of Europe's most prominent forces. Involved in many of the key conflicts of the era, against Russia, Ukraine, Sweden and the Ottoman Empire, the commonwealth was a pillar of European geopolitics. Yet, it gradually lost territory and clout during the 18th century, finally being portioned in 1795 by Prussia (the kingdom based in Berlin and which would be the cornerstone of a unified Germany in the 19th century), Austria and Russia.[1] Lithuania itself had gradually lost sway within the commonwealth itself as it found itself "Polonized." A class divide developed between the richer and more educated Poles and the agricultural Lithuanians. Although both Prussia and Austria took some Lithuanian territory in the annexations of 1795, the majority of the territory came under Russian control.

Tsarist Russia at the turn of the 19th century had an insatiable appetite for new land and power. The by now much diminished Lithuania was a minnow against the rapidly growing Russian Empire. The Tsarist regime was deeply authoritarian, brokering little dissent and clumsily attempting to exert its will over the peoples whose land it occupied. During the 19th century this heavy-handedness managed to fuel the burgeoning flames of Lithuanian nationalism. This was the era of cultural nationalism and Lithuanians had plenty of history to fall back on without needing to create national "myths," as many nations seemed to do during the century. The approach of Lithuanian nationalists, however, was unique and took a particular turn. The prime focus of its nationalism was the revival of the Lithuanian language, which had been suppressed even during the commonwealth era. This would mean breaking from a joint Polish-Lithuanian history that may have developed from 1569-1795. This was not always easy. Perhaps the best-known figure in 19th century Lithuanian nationalism was the poet Adam Mickiewicz (1798-1855), who managed to be a key figure in Lithuania, Poland and Belarus. Lithuanians agitated for greater recognition of culture and linguistic rights during the century. There were two major revolts, in 1831 and 1863, which were suppressed by the Russians, who sought to stifle both the Lithuanian language and the Catholic religion. Following the revolts, more serious attempts at "Russification" by the occupiers took place. Meanwhile, Lithuanian nationalists, some of whom had wanted to revive the joint commonwealth at the beginning of the 19th century, had by the end of the century taken a far more independent Lithuania stance. In practice this meant

---

[1] Brendan Simms, *Europe: The Struggle for Supremacy 1453 to the Present* (London: Penguin, 2014)

nationalists would focus on a much smaller area than the historic Grand Duchy of Lithuania or Polish-Lithuanian Commonwealth, abandoning any claims on Polish, Ukrainian and Belarusian territory.

At the turn of the 20th century, Lithuania had been ruled by Russia for over 100 years. In geopolitical terms, the 19th century, particularly after the Napoleonic Wars, had been relatively stable. Sometimes known as the Concert of Vienna (after the city where the post-Napoleonic wars peace settlement was negotiated), Europe's great powers had few wars in the following decades, with exceptions including the 1853-56 Crimean War and 1870-71 Franco-Prussian War. Yet, all was not well with great power relations in the first decade of the 20th century.[2] The likes of Russia and Germany were eager to expand their respective territories while Britain and France were more defensive, seeking to hold on to the huge empires they had amassed. The Ottoman and Austria-Hungary Habsburg empires were weakened, creating rivalries to annex land from their peripheries. Meanwhile, populations in occupied and colonized parts of these huge empires were agitating for change, greater recognition and even independence. Lithuania fell very much in these latter categories, with many of its people unhappy with a century of Russian rule.

With the hindsight of history, however, the Russian Empire at the turn of the 20th century was fragile. A popular revolution in 1905, when peasants and workers stormed the Tsar's Winter Palace, as well as a defeat in a war against the Japanese rattled the ruling Romanov dynasty sufficiently to offer some proto-democratic reforms, or at least greater power to the Russian parliament, the Duma. Ultimately, the reforms proved disappointing to the growing number of discontents within Russia and its empire, leading to socialist, anarchist, liberal and nationalist groups all agitating for change, if not outright revolution. In the Baltic states, the 1905 unrest increased demands for cultural self-determination, rather than outright sovereignty. The 1917 Russian Revolution, or more accurately two revolutions (the first in February and second in October), brought down Tsar Nicholas II and his regime, culminating in a takeover by the communist Bolsheviks led by Vladimir Lenin. It should be remembered, however, that during the first decade and a half of the century the Russian Empire was widely feared by its European rivals. The actions of Austria-Hungary and Germany in 1914 were predicated on the fact that they expected a Russian attack and that the Tsarist forces had proved generally formidable during the previous two centuries. The Russian Empire itself had allied itself with Britain and France before 1914, apparently forming a strong "Triple Entente."[3] In Lithuania, the early years of the 20th century continued much as the previous ones of the 19th century. The national revival centered on the Lithuanian culture and language, as well as the Catholic church. Whereas other European empires, such as Austria-Hungary and even Germany, could point to some gains for the inhabitants of peripheral areas, the same could hardly be said for Russia. Still to significantly industrialize, Russia and its empire was predominantly agricultural, consisting of a land-based peasantry with few rights. Holding some attractiveness to the rulers in St. Petersburg—the

[2] Dominic Lieven, *Towards the Flame: Empire, War and the End of Tsarist Russia* (London: Penguin, 2016)
[3] Christopher Clark, *The Sleepwalkers: How Europe Went to War in 1914* (London: Harper, 2014)

greatest resistance to imperial rule tended to emanate from industrial workers organizing in larger cities—Russia nevertheless could not provide the economic growth and benefits that may have pacified the inhabitants of occupied countries such as Lithuania. The tools the center relied upon were suppression, including a crackdown after the events of 1905, and Russification.

One of the results of the pre-1914 situation was mass emigration from Lithuania, some to other parts of the Russian Empire, such as the capital St. Petersburg, or further afield, notably the United States. Several waves of Lithuanian migrants moved to the US in the 19th century and then in the 1940s after Nazi and Soviet occupations. Today there are more than 650,000 descendants of Lithuanians in the US, with the biggest populations living in Pennsylvania and Illinois. In the early 20th century, the prospect of change, or even reform, in Lithuania seemed slim. The First World War would change all this, by shaking the kaleidoscope of the entire Central and Eastern Europe region, offering the possibility of independence and sovereignty for countries like Lithuania.

A sign of the weakening of Russia's grip on power in Lithuania before the First World War— as part of the Tsar's post-1905 reforms—was the relaxation of the use of the Lithuanian language, as well as restrictions on the Catholic church. Yet the Tsar was an unwilling reformer and when the chance came, he stalled on further progress.[4] The conflict that erupted in 1914 saw a clampdown on society and the mass mobilization of most of the empire to fight in the war. Meanwhile, a sign of things to come had been taking place in German-occupied Lithuania throughout the 19th century. Centerd around the coastal Klaipėda Region, the German Empire had "Germanized" the land annexed by Prussia in the late 18th century. Again, the Lithuanian language and its prohibition would prove focal points for nationalists. Nationalists were active in both Russian and German ruled portions of Lithuania. Crucially, that both larger powers had a foothold in Lithuania and coveted greater influence would mean the country would become embroiled in the 1914-1918 conflict.

The war that broke out in August 1914 had numerous causes, notably great power rivalry, and was played out in numerous theaters.[5] While the Western Front mainly took place in France and Belgium and was four years of grinding trench warfare, the Eastern Front was far more mobile and affected many smaller countries.[6] The impact of the war would mean liberation for several nations from larger empires, in keeping with President Woodrow Wilson's "14 Points" based on self-determination at the post-war Versailles Conference, while for others the conflict left a legacy of disquiet and injustice. The outcome of the war was still being fought until the outbreak of the Second World War in 1939. It was two such smaller states, Serbia and Bosnia-Hercegovina, which initially played a part in the start of the conflict. Serb nationalists assassinated the heir to the Austrian Empire, Archduke Franz Ferdinand, in Sarajevo in Bosnia in

---

[4] Sheila Fitzpatrick, *The Russian Revolution* (Oxford: Oxford University Press, 2008)
[5] Richard J. Evans, *The Pursuit of Power: Europe 1815-1914* (London: Penguin, 2017)
[6] Christopher Clark, *The Sleepwalkers: How Europe Went to War in 1914* (London: Harper, 2014)

June 1914. These Serb nationalists sought a "Greater Serbia" that would incorporate Bosnian territory, which itself had been recently annexed by an overextending Austrian Empire. The assassination led to a series of ultimatums from Austria on Serbia that led to war being declared by Vienna, setting in motion the great power defense agreements that pitted Russia, France and Britain against Austria-Hungary and Germany. For most Lithuanians this meant they would be forced into fighting on the Russian side of the conflict, in some cases against German-occupied Lithuania (sometimes called Lithuania Minor).

The protagonists in 1914 assumed, as with previous conflicts, any war would be a short one. The various war aims included gaining some territory or forcing concessions from other powers, to recognize other claims. For instance, France wanted to regain the Alsace-Lorraine region it had lost to Germany in the 1870-71 war, while Germany sought to consolidate its position there. Russia, meanwhile, wanted to expand its presence in the Balkan region. Britain sought to protect its trade routes and its naval hegemony. The Baltic region was also important. Tucked in the corner of the Baltic Sea between Scandinavia, south-eastern mainland Europe and the north-westerly corner of the huge Russian Empire, Estonia, Latvia and Lithuania were an important trading route as well as occupying a key geostrategic position. As a result, one of the secondary war aims of Germany and Russia was to gain control over the entire Baltic region.

The early stages of the First World War took place between Austria-Hungary and Serbia, followed by the former's armies against Russia in Eastern Europe, notably the region of Galicia. Germany was quickly drawn into the fighting on the eastern front of the war, proving much more difficult opponents for the Russians than the Habsburg armies. Yet, this action was in contradiction to the long-tabled German war strategy, the "Schlieffen Plan," which envisaged a quick victory in the west against France—including a swift offensive through Belgium—before fighting the more implacable Russian forces in the east.[7] It would not be long, however, that the fighting moved further north and incorporated the Baltic region.

After war was declared in 1914, as with most of the participating countries, the initial impact was a "rally round the flag" effect, or support for the ruling class. In Lithuania the press came out in fervent support of the Tsar and his regime's policy of war. This was partly war euphoria and partly anti-German sentiment. The German presence in Lithuania Minor, the Germanization attempts and the dominant role ethnic Germans were playing in the Baltics more generally, was causing disquiet. German authorities had also encouraged migration to the area during the previous decades. Therefore, Lithuanians were hostile to both Russian and German imperial projects, but at the start of World War One this was harnessed more towards the latter than the former. In addition, some Lithuanians thought that wholeheartedly supporting the Russian war effort might result in greater autonomy in the event of victory. Although in some respects Russian authorities were suspicious of the allegiances of some inhabitants of the empire, including the Baltics, they nevertheless drafted 120,000 Lithuanians to fight in the war.[8]

---

[7] Ibid.

One of the key themes of Lithuania's 20th century history is occupation. By some counts historians can consider five occupations in the century: 1900-15 by the Russian Empire, 1915-18 by the German Empire, 1940-41 by the Soviet Union, 1941-44 by the Nazis and 1944-91 again by the Soviets. The German army took control of Lithuania in 1915 and held it for the rest of the war. Launching a major offensive in May 1915, the Germans attempted successfully to take Warsaw, then the second largest Lithuanian city, Kaunas, in August, followed by the capital Vilnius in September. The German Empire called this captured territory "Ober Ost," or Upper East, which incorporated Lithuania and land further to the south. Most of Latvia to the north was outside Ober Ost. The Germans used Ober Ost as a military base for its operations on the Eastern Front; the military regime requisitioned materials and food and even used forced labour. German treatment of the local population was typically severe, preventing movement between different areas and generally treating Lithuanians with disdain, combined with a general racism towards the "east" and its peoples more broadly.[9] The Ober Ost regime was intent on further Germanizing Lithuania and made plain its intentions to pursue this policy if, as it expected, it won the war and then annexed the territory. As a result, many Lithuanians fled the country, for the most part into the surrounding region not occupied by Germany.

Unsurprisingly, the events of the war radicalized many Lithuanians. The early support for Russia had collapsed after the empire had failed to defend Lithuania from German attack and occupation. At the same time, Russian officers and the military high command were increasingly seen as inept. The centuries' old reputation of a formidable Russian army seemed to dissolve in a matter of months during World War I and played a crucial role in leading to the uprisings of 1917 that deposed the tsar, and Lithuanian nationalists sought to take matters into their own hands. In 1916 a group in Vilnius formed the "Taryba" (or Lietuvos Valstybės Taryba), the Lithuanian National Council. The Taryba declared its desire for self-determination.

Initially, the German authorities did not crack down on the national council and subsequently sought to use to Taryba to its advantage. Nevertheless, the council made its stance clear: whereas in other Baltic states there were discussions between nationalists over whether to seek greater autonomy within the larger empire or outright independence, the German occupation made the issue more straightforward for Lithuanians, who insisted the occupation had to end. This was formalized at the Vilnius Conference of September 1917, where the Lithuanian National Council officially designated itself as the flagbearers of the will of the Lithuanian people and declared that it sought a state independent of its larger neighbors, with culture and language as two of its core components. The conference also decided that future decisions, once a state had been formed, would be pursued through democratic means. The conference echoed other moves by smaller, occupied states in Central and Eastern Europe, which formed a key set of interests at the

---

[8] Baltic Information, "Baltic States In WWI", 17 June 2020, https://baltinfo.org/baltic-states-in-wwi/, [accessed 14 September 2020]

[9] Peter Gatrell, Vejas Liulevicius, "Review of War Land on the Eastern Front: Culture, National Identity, and German Occupation in World War I", *Slavic Review* (60 (4): 844–845, 2001).

1919 Versailles Peace Conference.[10] Nevertheless, the Vilnius Conference, governed by the 20-man council, laid out a remarkably progressive set of goals. Ethnic Germans would be granted autonomy in the Klaipeda region while the sizeable Jewish population would also be granted cultural autonomy. Only Poles received a hostile reception at the conference due to their claims on the city of Vilnius itself, an issue that would prove live in the interwar period. Although the 1917 conference may not have seemed to be meeting at a propitious moment, Lithuanians would see an opportunity to put some of the principles into practice in little more than a year.

The First World War fundamentally changed the situation in the Baltics. With the conflict still raging, another geopolitical earthquake struck: the 1917 Russian Revolution. The tsar was overthrown by widespread discontent in February that year, not least by the regime's handling of the war and the huge number of casualties, followed in October by a coup d'état headed by Bolsheviks led by Vladimir Lenin.[11] The revolution would come to impact Lithuania, but initially it would lead to the collapse of Russian forces on the eastern front and Lenin seeking to end the war and sign an armistice. The German army then took the opportunity to move further northwards into the Baltic region, capturing the Latvian capital of Riga in 1917.

---

[10] Godfrey Hodgson, *People's Century: From the dawn of the century to the eve of the millennium* (Godalming: BBC Books, 1998)
[11] Sheila Fitzpatrick, *The Russian Revolution* (Oxford: Oxford University Press, 2008)

Lenin

Lithuania Declares Independence

The period between the two Russian Revolutions of 1917 and their immediate aftermath were chaotic for the whole of the Russian Empire, including the Baltic region. Suddenly, numerous possibilities presented themselves, not least national self-determination and independence. Many nations within the empire would declare independence, often in tumultuous circumstances with several groups at once claiming authority over the same area. Lithuania too would declare its sovereignty but was in a slightly different situation because it was still being occupied by the Germans. In fact, the revolution enhanced Germany's position in the war and the Baltic region more generally. It would be reversed on the Western Front and the ultimate defeat in 1918 that would lead to its eventual retreat from Lithuania.

Meanwhile, Lenin's Bolsheviks (translating as the majority segment of the communists, the "Mensheviks" were the minority) only had a very fragile grip on power in 1917-18. Lenin's initial strategy was to set up a "dictatorship of the proletariat," whereby a central authority would guide and lead the revolution. In addition, while Lenin's right-hand man Leon Trotsky favored world revolution, the reality after the Bolsheviks took power was that the Russian Empire was in fact crumbling, and the Bolsheviks needed to establish power within this territory before they could export it. This fact would mean that the communist regime sought to end the war as soon as possible, install like-minded "Soviets" dominated by workers in the various republics of a new Soviet Union, or USSR (Union of Soviet Socialist Republics), and purge forces loyal to the tsar or opposed to the Bolsheviks. As a result, civil war erupted in 1918, and for the next four years there was a brutal struggle to impose communist control over the former Russian Empire, extinguishing renegade provinces and nations.

Trotsky

The Baltic states, however, would prove elusive to the Bolshevik regime as they sensed their first period of autonomy in the 20th century was in grasp, but for Lithuania, it would first need to push out the German occupiers in 1917-18.

The Soviet regime knew that dissatisfaction with the handling of the First World War had been a key component of its rise to , so when a provisional government took over after the February 1917 Revolution, it continued to prosecute the war. This gave the anti-war Bolsheviks the opportunity to seize power eight months later, and the Soviet government agreed to the Brest-Litovsk peace treaty in March 1918. It was highly favorable to the Germans, who after all had forced the Russians to seek terms, and the treaty handed over swathes of land to the Central Powers and surrendered territory formerly part of the Russian Empire.[12]

---

[12] Robert Gerwarth, *The Vanquished: Why the First World War Failed to End, 1917-1923* (London: Allen Lane, 2016)

The Brest-Litovsk settlement was never tested because the treaty was essentially torn up when the Germans signed an armistice in November 1918 after having been defeated on the Western Front by France, Britain and the new entrants, the United States. Nevertheless, the Baltic states again offered an exception from the general trend at the end of the war. The treaty cleaved the three Baltic states away from the Russian Empire and aligned them with Germany, under the "protection" of the German Kaiser. As part of the arrangement, Lithuania would be governed by an elite of the minority German population. Becoming desperate at the end of the war, the German authorities had even accepted the Taryba's declaration of autonomy in return for a permanent alliance with Berlin.

In February 1918, Lithuanian nationalists declared independence, initially as a democratic republic but then modified as a constitutional monarchy in the same format as the Grand Duchy. The Taryba saw the step as a compromise with the Germans by establishing independence while keeping the occupiers on side, and they invited a German noble, Wilhelm, 2nd Duke of Urach, to reign as King Mindaugas II. The German authorities acquiesced to the idea as a means of pacifying and securing the country, but the proposed monarch never arrived in Lithuania. The appointment had caused a division within the Lithuanian National Council and was particularly opposed by socialists on the left of the body. The German military authorities also refused to devolve power to a Lithuanian-led government, wanting to annex the country outright rather than support the plan agreed by politicians in Berlin. It was only in the final phase of the war that Germany changed its approach to Lithuania. Chancellor Max von Baden allowed Lithuanians to take over the country's administration, set up a republic (rather than constitutional monarchy), and establish a democratic system of governance.

The Duke of Urach

Baden

German influence over Lithuanian affairs became moot in November 1918. As the Kaiser's regime crumbled in Berlin, a republic was declared and an armistice signed with the protagonists on the Western Front. The German army then went into retreat in the east as well, and the Brest-Litovsk treaty lost its authority. Thus, even though Lithuania had declared independence earlier in 1918, it was not until the end of the conflict that it finally got to put this claim into practice.

A government was formed in November, and it began to legislate for events in Lithuania ahead of any forthcoming peace conference. A provisional constitution was drafted, basic state organs established, and Augustinas Voldemaras led Lithuania's first government starting in late 1918. A prominent Lithuanian nationalist who had previously lived in St. Petersburg, Voldemaras had joined the Lithuanian National Council earlier in the year, and along with being prime minister, he appointed himself as defense and foreign minister. Voldemaras was involved in the initial disputes over whether the country should have a military. As a largely pacifist country, which many states were expected to be in the aftermath of the First World War, some Lithuanian leaders thought there was no need for armed forces. This quickly changed as it became clear that the fledgling state faced aggression from every side.

Voldemaras

As a result, Voldemaras' urgent task at the end of 1918 was to secure the internal borders of Lithuania. When he left in December to join the other peace negotiators at Versailles, the very fact of his "abandoning" Lithuania in the face of likely Soviet invasion caused outrage. Voldemaras was replaced by Mykolas Sleževičius, who served as prime minister on three occasions between 1918-26.

I ir IV Ministerių Kabineto Pirnininkas, Steig Seimo narys, Soc .iaud. Dem. lyderis, pris. advokatas.	Prime Minister of the 2d and 4th cabinet: Member of the Constituent Assembly, sworn lawyer.

Sleževičius

From 1918-22, Lithuanian independence was violent and unstable. Lithuania was on the periphery of the Russian Civil War and Moscow wanted to impose communist rule. The Soviet Red Army did indeed invade Lithuania in 1919 but was, unlike most other combatants in the 20th century, actually repelled. Poland, which had regained its independence after the end of the First World War, coveted Lithuania either as a revived Polish-Lithuanian Commonwealth or outright annexation. Germany may have been defeated in 1918, but it was also reluctant to completely surrender its gains from the Brest-Litovsk treaty. It was also a constant presence in the region, and ethnic Germans retained influence in Lithuania, including the Klaipeda region, after 1918.

In the popular imagination, the aftermath of the First World War, known by many at the time as the "Great War," advanced in a number of discrete phases.[13] After the armistice in November

---

[13] Godfrey Hodgson, *People's Century: From the dawn of the century to the eve of the millennium* (Godalming: BBC Books, 1998)

1918, German forces were compelled to retreat back to Germany itself, where revolutionary forces were attempting to take power. As it turned out, a democratic government, the Weimar Republic, was established. Meanwhile, the victorious nations congregated at the Palace of Versailles near Paris from January 1919, as well as numerous smaller nations seeking autonomy from the German, Austria-Hungary and Ottoman Empires, to discuss a post-war settlement. The eventual outcome, the Treaty of Versailles, signed in June 1919, fundamentally changed borders and the balance of power in Europe, and was widely seen as punitive towards Germany. In hindsight, however, writers such as Robert Gerwarth in *The Vanquished: Why the First World War Failed to End, 1917-1923* have outlined how the situation in the East was far more fluid and confused. In many areas the fighting continued, governments were formed and toppled, and coups were launched with brutal fighting continuing into the early 1920s. Lithuania was one such example.[14]

One of the key problems for independent Lithuania was that it was caught up in the fighting in Russia as both pro-Bolshevik and pro-tsar forces fought against Lithuanian troops. Even more intractably, Poland pressed its claims on Lithuanian territory, in particular Vilnius and the surrounding area, and an independent Poland was one of the key topics at the Versailles negotiations and backed by the Western powers. As a result, Poland seemed to gain favorable treatment from the war's victors, including occupying Vilnius without sanction, much to the chagrin of the Lithuanians, who had to use Kaunas as their capital during the Interwar Period.

In fact, the Western powers did not recognize Lithuania as independent until 1922 despite the country being a subject for discussion at Versailles. Despite President Woodrow Wilson's "14 Points" and claims to be supporting national self-determination, Lithuania, which had spent centuries as an independent state and which had been clearly annexed by the Russians in 1795, was given short shrift at the 1919 peace conference. Represented by Augustinas Voldemaras, who continued as foreign minister despite being ousted as prime minister, and President Antanas Smetona, Lithuanian negotiators tried in vain to achieve recognition from the key decision makers at Versailles for their new state and its territorial integrity.[15] The main arguments against Lithuanian independence were those who supported a strong Russia to repel Germany in the future and those who favored Poland, which would thereby incorporate some or all of Lithuania. Voldemaras continued to push for recognition after the failure of Versailles, again unsuccessfully. It was only in 1922 that Lithuania finally achieved official great power recognition after a number of treaties.

---

[14] Robert Gerwarth, *The Vanquished: Why the First World War Failed to End, 1917-1923* (London: Allen Lane, 2016), 175.

[15] Godfrey Hodgson, *People's Century: From the dawn of the century to the eve of the millennium* (Godalming: BBC Books, 1998)

Smetona

The Interwar Period

As discussed earlier, the Lithuanian National Council set out a progressive set of principles at the 1917 Vilnius Conference as well as the independence declaration in 1918. Indeed, the first years of Lithuanian autonomy, despite numerous conflicts and external threats, were governed by democratically elected administrations. In practice, however, the young Lithuanian republic exhibited behaviours similar to many other European states at this time. For instance, Lithuanian troops invaded Klaipeda in January 1923, then still administered by the League of Nations under French military command. After mediation from the League, Lithuania annexed the region, promising to ensure the rights of non-Lithuanians, most significantly ethnic Germans, in a power sharing arrangement.

The invasion of Klaipeda came a year after the Western powers had recognized Lithuania's independence. This itself followed several years of conflict, culminating in the 1920 Treaty of Moscow and 1921 Treaty of Riga. The Soviet Red Army had invaded Lithuania in early 1919 and installed the "Socialist Soviet Republic of Byelorussia," which included Belarus. Nevertheless, Lithuanian forces, including some Germans, supported by Polish troops, pushed the Soviets out by September 1919; some feat considering the relative size of the armies. The situation became even more complicated in 1920. Although Lithuania and the Soviets had essentially ended hostilities, the Russians fought against Poland, while Lithuanians and Poles fought each other over control of the Vilnius region. At one stage it was the Russians that occupied Vilnius in 1920 but after losing the Battle of Warsaw, were forced to retreat, allowing the Poles to take the capital region. Lithuania would sign a peace agreement with the Soviets in October 1920, recognizing the former's independence in return for neutrality in Soviet affairs. The League of Nations put pressure on the Poles to negotiate the Suwalki Treaty, also in October 1920, signed in the town of Suwalki on the border between the two countries, which recognized the borders of Lithuania. While the League seemed to have notched up an early diplomatic success in brokering the deal, a sign of future failures was on show as the Poles violated the treaty and occupied Vilnius. The occupation was obviously deeply divisive and unwelcome for Lithuanians who were unable to reverse the move for the remainder of their interwar independence. As a result, the capital of Lithuania was Kaunas during this period. A further treaty, the 1921 Peace of Riga, was signed between Poland and the USSR on regional borders, but Lithuania was not offered concessions on the Vilnius occupation.

Despite its frustrations over recognition and borders, a new Lithuanian state had been established between 1918-22, now accepted by Europe's major powers. This, however, was somewhat of a contradiction in terms, as an independent Lithuania never exerted sovereignty over its capital city Vilnius during this period. Nevertheless, after the annexation of Klaipeda in 1923, which was supported by the League of Nations, Lithuania was now at highest point since the end of the war. This final issue, with a substantial ethnic German minority, would unfortunately make it—and Lithuania more widely—a target for German revisionism when the Nazis came to power in the 1930s. Klaipeda would occupy a position similarly to Danzig (today's Gdansk in Poland) and the Sudetenland in the northwestern region of Czechoslovakia: places with substantial German-speaking populations that the Nazis could use as pretexts for aggression, invasion, and annexation.[16] This was made more difficult for Lithuania's government when the League's "Conference of Ambassadors," one of the key international decision-making bodies in the 1920s, recognized the status quo in Vilnius in March 1923.

Democracy in Lithuania in the early years of independence was also problematic, partly due to different groups refusing to accept the post-1918 situation and partly because after elections were held, parliamentarians found it difficult to approve governments. The first official elections to the *Seimas* (parliament) were held in October 1922 with the center-right Christian Democrats

---

[16] Ibid.

gaining most seats, 38, but not enough to secure a majority in the 78-member chamber. Following the deadlock for a number of months new elections were held in May 1923, and this time the Christian Democrats won 40 seats and were therefore able to form a government, led by Ernestas Galvanauskas as prime minister, also re-electing Aleksandras Stulginskis as president. This second Seimas of the independent period made some gains, achieving some degree of economic stability, initiated some land reform and developed a social security system while expanding the provision of education. Successive governments, however, were fragile and repeatedly collapsed. During the 1923-26 session, Galvanauskas, Antanas Tumėnas, Vytautas Petrulis and Leonas Bistras all led short-lived governments. Political instability reflected the lack of acceptance of the Lithuanian state both internally and externally and the continuing tension around Vilnius.

As with so many other European states during the interwar period, the early optimism after 1918 that a peaceful, more representative, order would emerge became largely frustrated. This was primarily because of the weakness of the Treaty of Versailles and its associated international organization, the League of Nations. Many grievances were caused or unresolved by Versailles and the League proved incapable of dealing with the numerous issues that festered in the 1920s. The reality of the post-war period, the difficulty in making democracy work and coexisting with neighboring states, caused many countries to seek other options from the middle of the decade, notably authoritarianism. Lithuania was similar. In May 1926, the third Seimas was elected and this time the electorate turned against the ruling party. While the Christian Democrats remained the largest party, with 30 seats, a coalition of other parties—the Peasant Popular Union, Social Democrats and minority parties—formed a government, with Mykolas Sleževičius becoming prime minister for the third time and Kazys Grinius president.

The 1926 government was the first, and only, left of center arrangement truly democratically elected in the interwar period. It was not long until the conservative establishment started to rail against the Sleževičius administration and begin to plan to overthrow it. The main complaints against the government was that it was encouraging "Bolshevization" by emboldening left-wing forces and improving links with Moscow. Indeed, a non-aggression pact was signed with the Soviet Union in September 1926, but this had been agreed to by the Christian Democrat predecessor government. A number of communist-led protests did take place in several cities, perhaps reassured by what was considered a sympathetic government. In any case, by December 1926 conservatives felt sufficiently unhappy and threatened by the new regime that it organised a military coup against it. The forcible takeover took place on December 17, 1926, with Antanas Smetona appointed president and Augustinas Voldemaras returning as prime minister. Grinius was put under house arrest. Smetona and Voldemaras, both members of the Lithuanian National Union, attempted to put a democratic façade on the coup by reopening the parliament and seeking support for the government. When a populist group organised demonstrations against the authoritarian government in April 1927, it was met with arrests and a crackdown. This led to parliamentarians seeking a vote of no confidence, and Smetona dissolved the Seimas, which he was constitutionally able to do, and did not call fresh elections.

As a result, Smetona was essentially the unelected autocratic leader of Lithuania until the Second World War,[17] and in many ways he pursued familiar policies for the period. He cracked down on dissent, stifled political opposition, and boosted his Lithuanian National Union. While Voldemaras appeared to be an ally, repeatedly serving as prime minister, Smetona resented the former's increasing independent streak and ultimately forced him to resign. When ethnic German activists agitated for greater autonomy and against rule from Kaunas, Smetona reacted by imprisoning around 100 of the group's participants. Smetona also attempted some semblance of a cult of personality, expanding his powers and adopting the moniker "leader of the people."[18] The president also had somewhat of a simplistic view of economics, seeking self-sufficiency without engaging in foreign trade, particularly if it meant balance of payments deficits.

That said, not all of Smetona's policies were self-defeating or negative. Although Lithuania's economy was still largely agricultural-based during this time, industrial output, against a backdrop of a global economic depression, expanded by 350% between 1928-39.[19] Foreign debt was small and balance of payments remained in surplus for almost the entire period.[20] While Smetona's protectionist instincts probably prevented greater progress in Lithuania's interwar years, real gains were made. As one history of Lithuania put it, "The government compensated for the relative shortage of foreign investment by itself investing heavily in domestic enterprise, both cooperative and private. Under Smetona the state invested up to around 60 percent of the capital in joint stock companies, mainly in agricultural industries. Particularly important was the government's active role in modernizing the country's communications infrastructure-railways, roads, telecommunications and harbour facilities-after years of Russian indifference. Equally important were land reclamation projects in the countryside, such as the draining of swamp lands."[21]

One of the key developments for Lithuania was its orientation towards the West after over a century as part of the Russian Empire. The majority of the country's trade was with Germany, then Great Britain and Scandinavia, and when Lithuanian relations with Germany soured after the Nazis came to power, it turned even more to Britain as a trading partner. Overall though, while Smetona's rule clearly had authoritarian tendencies, independent Lithuania experienced significant economic development and social reform during its two decades of independence between the wars.

Into the 1930s, Lithuania still faced geopolitical challenges, not least the continuing issue of Vilnius. This would fade, however, when compared to the existential threats posed by Nazi

---

[17] Thomas Lane et al. *The Baltic States : Estonia, Latvia and Lithuania, Book 3*, (Taylor & Francis Group, 2002)
[18] Ibid, 12.
[19] Ibid, 11.
[20] Ibid, 12.
[21] Ibid, 12.

Germany and the Soviet Union.[22] Nevertheless, having been dominated by Russia for so long, Lithuania's primary concerns in the interwar period were with Germany over the Klaipeda region and Poland, with which relations were "poisoned" due to the Vilnius dispute.[23] In fact, the Soviets actually supported Lithuanian claims to Vilnius.

The balance of geopolitical power shifted once more after Adolf Hitler was appointed German chancellor in 1933 and the Nazis wasted little time in turning the country into a totalitarian dictatorship.[24] One of Hitler's policies that actually garnered significant support in Germany was his revisionism of the post-1918 borders. Lithuania's Klaipeda region and ethnic German minority would form part of this, initially saber rattling and subsequently efforts to forcibly change Europe's borders.

The Nazis would soon support anti-Lithuanian organizations in Klaipeda, partly leading to the aforementioned 1934 arrests. Berlin then declared a trade embargo on Lithuania as the Baltic state was gradually drawn into the contentious political vortex of the late 1930s. As Germany expanded its territory, invading the Rhineland, annexing Austria and then the Sudetenland, Lithuania became increasingly vulnerable. The final years of the decade saw an increasing number of compromises made in attempts to maintain, unsuccessfully, Lithuanian autonomy. Smetona's prestige was diminished by 1936 and he felt compelled to call elections, although these were hardly democratic: the number of seats was reduced to 49 and Smetona's Lithuanian Nationalists Union won 42 of these. The move was an attempt to increase Smetona's legitimacy, and he compounded the façade by writing a new constitution in 1938, passed by the supine Seimas.

Meanwhile, Poland offered Lithuania an ultimatum on March 17, 1938 to accept the territorial status quo or face war. It seemed that Warsaw, perhaps ironically in light of later events, had been emboldened by Nazi Germany's annexation of Austria and saw a chance to settle its own land disputes. The Lithuanian regime was cornered. Its international supporters were engaged in the failing appeasement strategy and were in no mood to support smaller states against larger aggressors, particularly in Lithuania's case, which had only reluctantly been recognized in 1922. The government reluctantly accepted the ultimatum in an attempt to avoid war. Worse was to come. One year later, on March 20, 1939, German Foreign Minister Joachim von Ribbentrop presented Lithuanian Foreign Minister Juozas Urbšys with a new ultimatum: cede the Klaipeda region or face invasion. Again, the Lithuanians were forced to acquiesce in the face of the huge German army, the Wehrmacht. Hitler had claimed the previous year that Klaipeda (known as the Memel region to Germans) was only eclipsed by the Sudetenland on his list of territorial targets.

---

[22] Godfrey Hodgson, *People's Century: From the dawn of the century to the eve of the millennium* (Godalming: BBC Books, 1998)

[23] Thomas Lane et al. *The Baltic States: Estonia, Latvia and Lithuania, Book 3 - Stepping Westwards*, (Taylor & Francis Group, 2002), 32.

[24] Godfrey Hodgson, *People's Century: From the dawn of the century to the eve of the millennium* (Godalming: BBC Books, 1998)

Urbšys

Ribbentrop

With Lithuania now being dismembered from all sides, it would only survive another few months before the grim years of the Second World War, when its people would fall prey to two barbarous totalitarian occupations, by the Nazis and Stalin's Soviet Union.

Occupation and Annexation

The final blow to Lithuania's independence came in August 1939 with the infamous Molotov–Ribbentrop Pact, a non-aggression agreement between the Nazis and the Soviets. This gave Hitler carte blanche to attack other European states, secure in the knowledge Stalin would not intervene. Only action from France and Britain would challenge Hitler's now unbridled desire for more land, but regardless, the pact was lethal for Lithuania, caught between the two dictators. Along with promising non-intervention in any war, the agreement divided up the countries between Germany and the USSR, notably Poland, and Lithuania was allocated to Germany.

The next month, September 1939, the Nazis invaded Poland and expected Lithuania to join them due to the long-running dispute over Vilnius. Smetona, however, refused to participate in the invasion. With surprisingly stiff resistance mounted by the Polish army, the situation in the Baltics became more fluid. The Soviet Red Army moved into the region, offering "mutual assistance" pacts to Estonia, Latvia, and Lithuania in exchange for stationing troops in the countries. Of course, this essentially amounted to Soviet military occupation, and Moscow would step up its pressure on Lithuania as the war progressed.

The Second World War would prove catastrophic for Lithuania, a country that officially did not participate in the conflict. After any semblance of international rules and norms broke down in the 1930s with the demise of the League of Nations, Lithuania was a pawn caught between two stronger powers. It had the misfortune to be invaded and occupied by both Nazi Germany and the Soviet Union, and when the dust settled in 1945, it would find itself again unrecognized by the League's successor, the United Nations (UN). The UN would attempt to give more weight to the superpowers rather than the more egalitarian League of Nations, and for Lithuania, this meant its acceptance as a republic of the USSR. Indeed, it would remain behind the Iron Curtain for 45 years.

After its pact with Stalin, Lithuania did achieve some brief respite from the war's early hostilities, but this changed after the Red Army concluded its war with Finland, which had rejected a mutual assistance pact, to the north. Stalin's next move was to present Smetona's regime with yet another ultimatum in June 1940. This time the Lithuanians had to accept a pro-Soviet communist puppet government or face invasion, even as Soviet troops were already stationed in the country. Smetona fled Lithuania and a "people's government" was formed, headed by Justas Paleckis under the supervision of Soviet representative Vladimir Dekanozov, while Lithuania was swiftly converted into a Soviet Socialist Republic and adopted into the USSR itself. While the Western Allies, Britain and France, were engaged in an existential fight with Nazi Germany in Western Europe, Stalin had moved to quietly annex more territory.

Paleckis

Within the country itself, events took a typically Stalinist turn during the rest of 1940 and 1941. The puppet regime sought to nationalize property and collective land while imprisoning and torturing real, possible or imagined opponents. In keeping with persecution in other parts of the Soviet empire, thousands of Lithuanians were deported to labor camps in other parts of the USSR, often in Siberia. Most never returned. There were also massacres in Lithuania itself, notoriously at Rainiai and Cherven, where more than 1,000 people were killed.

In June 1941 the Nazis launched "Operation Barbarossa," the secret attack against the Soviet Union that betrayed the 1939 non-aggression pact.[25] Hitler sought "Lebensraum" (living space) for the Third Reich and had a long-standing animosity against communists and people from Eastern Europe, especially the Slavs and the Soviet regime. Stalin was taken completely by surprise and the Soviet defenses were swept aside by the rampant Wehrmacht.

---

[25] Ibid.

Lithuania was close to the front line of Operation Barbarossa, and like many other republics of the USSR, many Lithuanians initially welcomed the Germans as "liberators," although this view would rapidly change. For Lithuanians this was further complicated by the previous tensions with ethnic Germans over the Klaipeda region. Nevertheless, an anti-Soviet uprising in June 1940 was launched by Lithuanian nationalists, who declared independence and formed a provisional government. Inevitably, this proved short-lived – the Wehrmacht had taken control of all Lithuanian territory by the end of June 1941, nullified the provisional government, and set up its own military administration. Lithuanians now found themselves occupied by Germans for the second time in the 20th century.

If the Soviet occupation had been grim, the Nazis would inflict further horrors on the country from 1941-44. Initially, some Lithuanians welcomed the German army, seeing it as a preferable alternative to the Soviets and even as a steppingstone to more autonomy. Some even willingly collaborated with the Germans and joined army units. It would not be long, however, that opinions changed towards the Nazis. Whereas the Nazis and many Lithuanians could agree on wanting to kick out the Soviets, in reality there were few other points of convergence. Indeed, Hitler saw Lithuania as merely a colony, and the occupying regime imposed brutal repression on the Lithuanian population.

For Lithuanian Jews, the consequences of the German invasion were far worse. From the earliest days of the invasion, German soldiers started to execute the Jewish population, which totaled up to 250,000 before the war. The Nazis managed to murder approximately 90% of Lithuania's Jews during the occupation through mass executions in 1941, confining them ghettos during 1942-43, and killing them in death camps from 1943-44. The brutality visited upon Lithuania's Jews was among the most barbarous of the war. The Jewish community in Lithuania had existed for hundreds of years, in particular focused in Vilnius, and the Nazis managed to almost eradicate it in less than four years.

The Second World War turned gradually in 1942-43 and then dramatically in 1944 as the Wehrmacht suffered defeats in the drawn-out fighting in the Soviet Union and then could not repel the allied landings in France in 1944. The war, however, was far from over, and it required the Red Army to drive the Nazis back to Germany through attritional and bloody warfare. At the same time, many scores were settled following German atrocities. A Lithuanian resistance movement emerged in 1943 and embraced the principles of the recently signed Atlantic Charter, therefore making it broadly pro-Western in nature. Indeed, there is some evidence that despite the horrors of Nazi occupation, Lithuanians still opposed the USSR more than Germany.[26]

Inevitably, however, it would be the Red Army that would "liberate" Lithuania as part of its sweep westwards in 1944, having almost total control by that September. This time, the Soviets were here to stay, and it was the peculiarly terrible fate of the Baltic states was experience not

---

[26] Ibid, 59.

one but three successive occupations, the object of which was, as the Committee of Liberation predicted, the destruction of the Lithuanian identity and the complete integration of the Lithuanian republic into the Soviet Union.[27]

The Second World War ended in Europe in May 1945 and in the Pacific in August 1945. For Lithuania, the conflict was essentially over officially in 1944 when the Red Army pushed out the Nazis. Nevertheless, Lithuanian partisans took up arms to repel the Soviet occupiers. The insurgency continued for several years and by some counts more Lithuanians died fighting in the post-war years than during the Second World War itself, by some estimates 30,000 combatants.

While the international community, such as it was in 1945, established the UN at the end of the war, there would be no Versailles-style peace conference attempting to balance the claims of individual countries. The 1945 Yalta and Potsdam conferences were exercises in great power diplomacy and hard-nosed calculation, and the results were that Lithuania and the other Baltic states were incorporated into the Soviet Union with little discussion. Indeed, Stalin now occupied most of the countries of Central and Eastern Europe, setting up pro-Moscow communist proxies in them and establishing the Cold War.[28] The superpower rivalry was made more precarious by the advent of nuclear weapons. Lithuania would find itself at the crucible of the tensions between East and West, positioned close to the border of the Iron Curtain itself.

In Lithuania, the Soviets pursued policies familiar to other parts of the Soviet Union during this period, most notably repression, the forced labor camps of the Gulag, and deportations. As with other areas of the USSR, such as Crimea and Chechnya, whole families were forcibly moved to other territories, and it is estimated that more than 100,000 Lithuanians were deported in the 1940s and early 1950s.

Naturally, some resisted, and the peak of the Lithuanian partisan insurgency occurred between 1946-48, mainly engaged in clandestine activities rather than open engagement with the Soviet military administration. Known as "Forest Brothers," the experiences of the partisans' insurgency were documented by exiled fighter Juozas Lukša, or Daumantas, in the memoir *Fighters for Freedom. Lithuanian Partisans Versus the U.S.S.R.*[29] Daumantas returned to Lithuania in 1950 but was killed the following year. The insurgency was eventually defeated by the Soviet secret police by 1953.

After almost 30 years as the totalitarian ruler of the USSR, Stalin died in March 1953. The post-war period for many Soviet republics, including new ones such as Lithuania, was one of acute Stalinization. In reality this meant severe repression, forced collectivization, attempts at industrialization, and dogmatic economic planning. Stalin wanted the Moscow-led bloc to

[27] Ibid, 59.
[28] Mark Gilbert, *Cold War Europe: The Politics of a Contested Continent* (Rowman & Littlefield, 2014)
[29] Juozas Daumantas, *Fighters For Freedom. Lithuanian Partisans Versus the U.S.S.R.* (translated by E. J. Harrison, New York: Manyland Books, 1975, originally published 1950)

operate in a system of autarchy, with few trading relationships with the outside world, and since most of the occupying Soviet forces and civilian administration spoke no Lithuanian, the Russian language was imposed on the population.[30] Perhaps one of the most surprising developments during the entire Soviet period was that despite attempts to suppress Lithuanian culture, language, and the Catholic Church, Lithuanian national identity survived. In cities such as Vilnius, it actually expanded. This would serve as a basis for Lithuanian nationalists to work from when independence finally returned in the 1990s.

When Stalin died, a relaxation occurred across the entire Soviet sphere of influence, particularly when Nikita Khrushchev emerged as its new leader. Repression was partly rolled-back, the Gulag was emptied, and there was even space for economic reform. Lithuania was in somewhat of a unique position - it was not outside the USSR itself like Hungary, where a degree of political openness was tolerated, but it was not as consolidated into the Soviet Union as other republics. This occasionally led to some wariness from Moscow over developments in the Baltic states as well as more of a disconnect. Overall, for Lithuania this meant a partial thaw in the 1950s in terms of cultural life, but, as with so many other parts of the communist bloc, this started to reverse after only a few years. By the end of the 1950s, Khrushchev began to reassert Russian hegemony over Lithuania.[31] Part of Moscow's Sovietization strategy was to encourage ethnic Russians to immigrate into the Baltic states.

---

[30] Thomas Lane et al. *The Baltic States: Estonia, Latvia and Lithuania, Book 3 - Stepping Westwards*, (Taylor & Francis Group, 2002), 60.
[31] Ibid, 68.

Khrushchev

Khrushchev was deposed in 1964 after what was considered by hardliners as his calamitous handling of the previous year's Cuba Missile Crisis, when the superpowers stood at the precipice of a nuclear exchange. He was replaced by Leonid Brezhnev, who ushered a more stable era for most parts of the Soviet Union. From the mid-1960s until the late 1970s, life in the USSR settled into a somewhat repetitive, even dull rhythm. Yet there was full employment, living standards slowly improved and the international picture looked calmer, at least from Moscow's perspective. This era was later derided by one of Brezhnev's successors, Mikhail Gorbachev, as one of stagnation. Certainly, many of the negative features of the Soviet model—repression, omnipotent propaganda, corruption and disappointing economic growth—continued during the Brezhnev years. Yet, compared to the periods both before and after, for many Soviet citizens these were years of welcome normality. Lithuania became to some extent a Soviet republic like many others, with factories supplying jobs, cities covered in post-war blocks of flats and brutalist architecture and numerous parades and events celebrating communism and Soviet achievements more generally.

Nevertheless, disquiet would emerge during the Brezhnev period. Major decisions were taken in Moscow on Lithuanian affairs and its economy. This dynamic would lead to frustration in many republics, bubbling above the surface in the Gorbachev era. As previously noted,

Lithuanian nationalism lived on despite the tsunami of communist propaganda. Vilnius became the hub of the nationalist movement, although this was still under the radar into the 1980s. Nevertheless, there were indications about the demands for change in the 1970s. The superpowers, along with European countries, signed the Helsinki Final Act in 1975, which guaranteed the continent's post-1945 borders as well as making some provisions for Human Rights. The latter issue would prove a long-term thorn in the side of communist countries. Lithuanians, with increasing contact with Western countries in the 1970s, started to demand Human Rights recognition.[32] There would also be concerns over the fate of Lithuanian language and culture after decades of Sovietization. These issues would surface more significantly in the 1980s.

From 1950-80, Lithuania was a Soviet republic essentially pacified by Moscow's rule. The century's more tumultuous events would take place before and after this era. When Leonid Brezhnev died in 1982, the USSR went through new leaders at an alarming pace. Brezhnev's successor Yuri Andropov died in 1984, and then Konstantin Chernenko suffered the same fate in 1985. The Soviet politburo, understandably, turned to a younger man to steady the ship: Mikhail Gorbachev. Perhaps the key figure in global politics during the 1980s, Gorbachev set about transforming both the Soviet system and the Cold War itself. His reforms would have almost immediate impact in Lithuania, and the other Baltic states, setting them on a rapid road to independence.

---

[32] Ibid, 94.

Gorbachev

The issue of Lithuanian autonomy was one where Gorbachev's reputation as a peaceful and reasonable Soviet leader slipped after he deployed the Red Army in the republic, but Gorbachev's goals were to boost the Soviet economy and reform the communist system, not overturn it. Aware when he took office that the USSR had overextended itself with foreign military adventures and that a deep malaise had taken hold in his country by the mid-1980s, Gorbachev took an unlikely approach: political reform to stimulate greater economic productivity. His flagship policy was *Glasnost* or openness. Whereas for years the Soviet population had been forced to conceal its real thoughts and complaints about the regime, Gorbachev now encouraged honest discussion and dialogue. It was a variation on the "Prague Spring" approach in Czechoslovakia in 1968 (violently put down by Soviet-led forces) that was dubbed "socialism with a human face." In foreign affairs Gorbachev reduced international tensions with the United States, signing a number of arms control treaties and, most surprising of all, pulled Soviet forces out of Central and Eastern Europe, declaring at the United Nations in 1988 that these countries could decide on their future path. Lithuania was suddenly no longer on the front line of the Cold War, which drew to a close in 1989-91. The fall of the Berlin Wall in November 1989 was emblematic of the conflict's demise.

Gorbachev was so confident in his political system that, given the choice, he thought people in it would choose variations on Soviet-style communism. Many Soviet citizens, however, had other ideas. Glasnost initially stimulated discussions around reform as well as some enthusiasm for previously banned books, art and other works. Complaints soon grew however and many took the opportunity to air grievances against the status quo. Subsequently, the new atmosphere allowed topics to be discussed that had been previously completely off limits, such as linguistic concerns, cultural nationalism and faith.[33] This even developed into wider nationalist claims and ultimately, succession and independence. Lithuania was at the center of how Glasnost developed into calls for independence from the Soviet Union, setting off a chain of events that would lead to the disintegration of the USSR itself. In 1988, as with so many of the other "Popular Front" groups, intellectuals and artists led by musician Vytautas Landsbergis were at the forefront of setting up a movement—the Lithuanian Movement for Reconstruction (Sajudis)—to further nationalist claims. Sajudis organised a rally in Vilnius against the "illegal occupation" of Lithuania by the Soviets. Sajudis, it should be noted, also contained many reformers, as opposed to radicals.[34] Nevertheless, the independence strain gained prominence through a number of demonstrations in 1988 and 1989. Gorbachev was somewhat taken by surprise by the nationalist challenge to Soviet rule and seemed initially unsure how to respond. The communist party leader in Lithuania, Ringaudas Songaila, was replaced by Algirdas Brazauskas. In a further attempt to quell growing demands in the republics, Gorbachev overhauled the USSR's political system in

---

[33] CNN, *Cold War* (TV Series, produced by Jeremy Isaacs and Pat Mitchell, 1998)

[34] Thomas Lane et al. *The Baltic States: Estonia, Latvia and Lithuania, Book 3 - Stepping Westwards*, (Taylor & Francis Group, 2002), 92.

1989, establishing an elected chamber, the Congress of People's Deputies. The body, however, was filled with increasingly nationalist politicians. Gorbachev, having set these events in motion with Glasnost, now appeared powerless to hold back the forces it had unleashed. On August 23, 1989 the "Baltic Way," a human chain stretching for almost 700 kilometers through all three Baltic states, showed the strength of feeling and for reform as well as autonomy. Around two million people participated in the Baltic Way demonstration.

The Sajudis took a step-by-step approach to greater autonomy, combining political guile with the now burgeoning nationalism. Lithuanian reformers would quote Article 76 of the Soviet constitution that each republic had an "obligation" to ensure comprehensive economic development, thereby demanding more say over economic policy.[35] Moscow surprisingly conceded to this demand in the summer of 1989, enacting the change in January 1990. Lithuanian nationalists had made their breakthrough and would now move headlong towards outright independence. Furthermore, the Baltic people's movements were inspiring likeminded groups across the USSR, notably in the Caucasus.

Independence Again

Along with granting the Lithuanian Soviet Republic more control over its economic affairs, the country had the opportunity to elect members of its "Supreme Soviet," essentially a national parliament that was usually made up of appointed communist apparatchiks. Gorbachev, however, in a further attempt to bolster representation, democratized these elections across the Soviet Union in early 1990. The Sajudis played a key role in the election, not by fielding candidates but by backing those it considered supportive of its aims. Of the 135 representatives elected to the Seimas, 91 were backed by the Sajudis. The ploy worked insofar as the vast majority of new parliamentarians supported Lithuanian independence, with the exception of the Soviet-backed communist party, which only won seven seats. On March 11, 1990, Sajudis leaders Vytautas Landsbergis was elected leader of the Supreme Soviet, which Landsbergis then abolished. Lithuania's independence was then declared.

---

[35] Ibid, 98.

Landsbergis

Gorbachev was taken by surprise by events. He had permitted the first democratic elections in the USSR's history and at the first opportunity, a republic had used them to try and break away from Moscow. Gorbachev himself had just been made president of the Soviet Union, a new role from the previous communist General Secretary that had ruled the federation. Nevertheless, Gorbachev had a hard-won reputation for pluralism and seeking to reduce tensions, rather than escalate it. During his tenure as Soviet leader, Gorbachev had ended the war in Afghanistan, started to reduce nuclear weapon stockpiles and withdraw troops from Central and Eastern Europe. To now act aggressively towards a Soviet republic, particularly when the republics were nominally part of federation, would go against the grain of Gorbachev's core policies. Yet, he was also under increasing pressure to move to stop succession by the hardliners in the politburo and the military, as demonstrated by the failed coup in August 1991.[36] Gorbachev's compromise solution was to impose sanctions on the recalcitrant republic shortly after the declaration of

---

36 Stephen White, *Communism and its Collapse* (Routledge, 2002), CNN, *Cold War* (TV Series, produced by Jeremy Isaacs and Pat Mitchell, 1998)

independence. Local units of the Red Army became more active and seized some public buildings. A "provisional government" was formed. Yet, for the most part, in 1990 the situation was one of uneasy calm. Meanwhile, Western countries started to put pressure on Moscow to recognize Lithuania's independence. More Soviet republics followed with declarations of their own. The Soviet empire was visibly tottering.

Finally, Gorbachev acted in January 1991 to bring breakaway Lithuania under Moscow's control. Following an announcement on January 10 demanding all independence statutes be overturned, Gorbachev agreed to a Red Army unit moving on Vilnius the following day, and then other Lithuanian cities. The focal point for the army's attacks became the television tower in Vilnius, one of the strategic buildings that many civilians had encircled in attempts to protect from seizure. On January 13, troops opened fire on crowds near the tower, killing 14 and injuring hundreds. International condemnation followed and calls for Lithuanian independence grew.

The Red Army continued to occupy the country for several months but there was no return to the actions of January 11-13. This was not the full-throated and brutal crackdowns that had occurred in the suppression of uprisings in Hungary in 1956 or Czechoslovakia in 1968. By 1991, the Soviet Union was in somewhat of a chaotic position and Gorbachev's leadership was weakening.[37] On February 9, 1991, an independence referendum was held in Lithuania with 90% voting for independence on an 85% turnout. For another six months, a tense stalemate prevailed. Vytautas Landsbergis was considered the legitimate head of government by Lithuanians but lack of recognition from the international community and the reluctance of Moscow to relinquish any of its republics left Vilnius in somewhat of a limbo position. It would be events at the highest echelons of the Soviet structure itself that would finally liberate Lithuania and the other Baltic states.

Hardliners in the Soviet military high command, as well as the ruling Politburo, had been frustrated for some time about the direction of the country under Mikhail Gorbachev. Feted abroad, Gorbachev was despised by some at home over his emollient foreign policy and counterproductive Glasnost initiative. With nationalism rife in many republics and the economy on its knees throughout the USSR, a motley crew of hardline communists and military leaders launched a coup against Gorbachev in August 1991. All the usual mechanisms were in place: Gorbachev had been detained at his summer dacha, apparently ill, and a "junta" made public statements after it captured state television. On this occasion, however, the Soviet population would themselves resist the coup. Led by Boris Yeltsin, who was trying to reawaken Russian nationalism, protestors demonstrated outside government buildings in Moscow. With the atmosphere febrile, the leaders of the coup backed down and reinstated Gorbachev. Nevertheless, by now fatally weakened politically, Gorbachev spent the rest of 1991 essentially in office but only partially in power. He was painfully aware that he owed his position to Yeltsin, who was himself trying to ride the tiger of nationalism. As a result, republics and sub-regions further

---

[37] Stephen White, *Communism and its Collapse* (Routledge, 2002)

pushed for independence throughout the USSR. With resistance towards national self-determination now reduced, the way was set for Lithuania to finally break free of the Soviet project. On September 6, 1991, the independence of Lithuania was recognized by Moscow and then the United Nations.[38] The USSR staggered on until the end of the year, when it was dissolved by Gorbachev, to be replaced by 15 successor states.

Not surprisingly, the 1990s were a heady decade. Whereas many post-Soviet states descended into civil war, disputes over borders and ultimately the reimposition of hegemony from Moscow, Lithuania acted quickly to orientate itself with Western Europe. In October 1992, a new constitution was drafted that was then approved by referendum. The document enshrined principles such as Human Rights, minority rights and a constitutional court. Perhaps most significantly, it set up a new role for a president with considerable powers, who would then have the power to appoint prime ministers and governments. In short, Lithuania's constitution shared similar traits to other European liberal democracies. The first elections after the new constitution was implemented were held in October 1992 but surprisingly Sajudis-backed candidates were beaten by the rebranded communists, the Democratic Labour Party of Lithuania (LDDP), who formed a coalition government. The result had much to do with rapid economic reforms that were taking place in the 1990s, particularly the disappointing outcomes of land reform. Apart from agriculture, Lithuania engaged in a widespread overhaul of its economy and transition to market-based arrangement, assisted by the likes of the International Monetary Fund. During the early to mid-1990s, a broad-reaching privatization programme was effected, as well as tax reform, a revalued currency (the litas), institutional changes and incentivization for private enterprise.[39] As with every other post-communist state, the 1990s' "structural adjustment" encouraged by the West led to many problems, from price rises to long-term unemployment and even penury. For societies used to full employment at the same place of work for potentially an entire career and rationed food and consumer goods, the 1990s came as somewhat of a shock, both culturally and financially. Yet, Lithuania weathered these changes better than some of its contemporaries, achieving solid growth and attracting significant investment by the 1990s. Apart from economic changes, the Baltic state made dramatic geopolitical changes during the decade.

Lithuania joined the Council of Europe in 1993, the same year Russian troops finally exited the country. These moves would have profound effects for the security and geopolitics of the country. Clearly, the departure of Moscow's forces meant, however temporarily, Lithuania was no longer under the military sway of Russia or within its security bloc. This came at a time when the new Russian Federation was itself in turmoil, with a collapsing economy, the rise of oligarchs and political chaos. Perhaps even more crucially, joining the Council of Europe meant adopting European "values" of Human Rights, democracy and respect for the rule of law. Joining

---

[38] European Parliament, "Lithuania and the Enlargement of the European Union", Briefing, https://www.europarl.europa.eu/enlargement/briefings/11a2_en.htm, [accessed 13 September 2020]

[39] Thomas Lane et al. *The Baltic States: Estonia, Latvia and Lithuania, Book 3 - Stepping Westwards*, (Taylor & Francis Group, 2002), 177.

the Council of Europe put Lithuania on the road to joining the burgeoning European Union itself.

Capitalizing on the direction of travel, Lithuania signed a "Treaty of Friendship" with Poland the following year, which was highly symbolic following the difficulties over Vilnius in the interwar period, and joined NATO's Partnership for Peace programme. The first decision pacified the relationship between two countries that Western European countries were keen to bring into their orbit. The second was important for bringing the Baltic states into the European security pact, further creating a new European zone of peace. This was followed in 1997 with a cooperation treaty with Russia that settled border disputes and normalized relations. Vilnius eventually joined NATO as a full member in 2004. This last development, joining NATO, was perhaps the most remarkable of the entire independence period so far. As a member of the alliance, Lithuania could rely on the United States' security umbrella, acting as a deterrent for any further Russia (or other) aggression. Moscow has shown itself to be fiercely opposed to any former Soviet states joining, or even vaguely aligning, with NATO. The three Baltic states are the only ones to have joined NATO and as a result, can truly be said to have left Russia's orbit. This was part good fortune, Russia was much weakened in the 1990s, and part of its own volition, acting quickly and effectively reforming and aligning with Western European countries.

Lithuania's security has run alongside economic success. As part of the pro-Western package and after the sacrifices involved in the transition period, Lithuania has managed to access EU markets and receive associated investment. Macroeconomic stability was achieved by pegging the litas to the US dollar from 1994 and the new European currency, the Euro, from 1992. Lithuania signed an association agreement with the EU in 1998, putting it on course to join as a full member, also giving it favored trading status. Lithuania joined the EU in 2004, along with nine other countries. The rapid growth of its economy has been astounding in the post-independence years. The average wealth of a Lithuanian, GDP per capita, increased from $2,300 in 1995 to $19,000 in 2018. To compare with its contemporaries, in the mid-1990s former Soviet countries Russia ($2,600) and Belarus ($1,400) recorded similar figures while neighbor Poland's average GDP per capita was closer to $4,000. In 2018 Lithuania was well ahead of these countries, with Poland around $15,000, Russia $11,000 and Belarus $6,000.[40] It has not all been plain sailing for Lithuania in its post-1991 development. For instance, a political scandal in the mid-1990s caused its two largest commercial banks to collapse and brought down a prime minister. Other scandals have occurred and yet, the broad trajectory of independent Lithuania within the EU's orbit, has been a successful, peaceful, and prosperous one.

Conclusion

The story of Lithuania for much of the 20th century was one of frustration and dashed hopes of independence, dominated mainly by Russia and also Germany, until the surprisingly rapid fall of the Soviet Union in 1990-91, when the Baltic state finally achieved autonomy. The swift

---

[40] Source: The World Bank.

progress towards European Union membership and orientation towards the West in the 1990s and 2000s was as dramatic as it was surprising. The optimistic coda to our story should not detract from the struggles of the rest of the century and the defiance required from the Lithuanian population to maintain its cultural and national identity throughout the period's many trials. As Lane et. al's history of the Baltic states explained, "For 70 years of the 20th century Lithuania has been occupied by a succession of repressive regimes. Through its extraordinary powers of resistance it has preserved its identity and recaptured its independence, but only after the most painful experience of terror, persecution, tyranny and personal tragedies."[41]

The journey of the small Baltic state from being dominated by major powers to winning independence after over a century of oppression was the kind of story in modern history that many other nations share, but Lithuania again faces a renewed challenge from its stronger neighbor to the East. That said, today Lithuania seems as secure and independent as it has in centuries, a fitting conclusion for a state that managed to withstand the major events of the 20th century and emerge in relative security and prosperity.

Online Resources

Other books about 20th century history by Charles River Editors

Other books about Lithuania on Amazon

Further Reading

Baltic Information, "Baltic States In WWI", 17 June 2020, https://baltinfo.org/baltic-states-in-wwi/

Christopher Clark, *The Sleepwalkers: How Europe Went to War in 1914* (London: Harper, 2014)

CNN, *Cold War* (TV Series, produced by Jeremy Isaacs and Pat Mitchell, 1998)

Juozas Daumantas, *Fighters For Freedom. Lithuanian Partisans Versus the U.S.S.R.* (translated by E. J. Harrison, New York: Manyland Books, 1975, originally published 1950)

European Parliament, "Lithuania and the Enlargement of the European Union", Briefing, https://www.europarl.europa.eu/enlargement/briefings/11a2_en.htm

Richard J. Evans, *The Pursuit of Power: Europe 1815-1914* (London: Penguin, 2017)

Sheila Fitzpatrick, *The Russian Revolution* (Oxford: Oxford University Press, 2008)

Peter Gatrell, Vejas Liulevicius, "Review of War Land on the Eastern Front: Culture, National Identity,

---

[41] Thomas Lane et al. *The Baltic States: Estonia, Latvia and Lithuania, Book 3 - Stepping Westwards*, (Taylor & Francis Group, 2002), 59.

and German Occupation in World War I", *Slavic Review* (60 (4): 844–845, 2001).

Robert Gerwarth, *The Vanquished: Why the First World War Failed to End, 1917-1923* (London: Allen Lane, 2016)

Mark Gilbert, *Cold War Europe: The Politics of a Contested Continent* (Rowman & Littlefield, 2014)

Godfrey Hodgson, *People's Century: From the dawn of the century to the eve of the millennium* (Godalming: BBC Books, 1998)

Thomas Lane et al. *The Baltic States: Estonia, Latvia and Lithuania, Book 3*, (Taylor & Francis Group, 2002)

Dominic Lieven, *Towards the Flame: Empire, War and the End of Tsarist Russia* (London: Penguin, 2016)

Brendan Simms, *Europe: The Struggle for Supremacy 1453 to the Present* (London: Penguin, 2014)

Stephen White, *Communism and its Collapse* (Routledge, 2002)

Free Books by Charles River Editors

We have brand new titles available for free most days of the week. To see which of our titles are currently free, click on this link.

Discounted Books by Charles River Editors

We have titles at a discount price of just 99 cents everyday. To see which of our titles are currently 99 cents, click on this link.

www.ingramcontent.com/pod-product-compliance
Lightning Source LLC
Chambersburg PA
CBHW081403160726
48000CB00010B/3464